1000
Folds

Joe Ross

chax press

ISBN 978-0-9894316-7-5
Printed and Bound in USA

Front Cover Design by Michael Fitzpatrick

Published by Chax Press
411 N 7th Ave Ste 103
Tucson AZ 85705-8388
USA

Ce pli de sombre dentelle, qui retient l'infini, tissé par mille, chacun selon le fil ou prolongement ignoré son secret, assemble des entrelacs distants où dort un luxe à inventorier, stryge, noud,feuillages et présenter.

Avec le rien de mystère, indispensable, qui demeure, exprimé, quelque peu.

L'Action Restreinte, Stéphane Mallarmé

    *   *   *   *   *   *

This fold of somber lace, which retains the infinite, woven by a thousand, each according to the thread or extension not knowing its secret, assembles the distant interlaced strands, there a sleeping luxury to inventory – strix, knot, foliage – and present.

With the void of mystery, indispensable, which remains expressed, somewhat.

— trans. Guy Bennett and Jim Wine

for *Juliette*

(the effort of breath)

Prologue

Edges constructed as a lark

in the making
sagging under a wing

                      was found to be
                      another wing

The world – in flight

                      fleeing

The description
from decapitation

           Delicate, this . . . .   under

                          taking

form – This marking

Into sickness or a saddle near a tearing
of joy — What the monarch

           ordered, in between invasions

Jumps then joins in at the reunions

           Lavish in pumps a ball, the room
Out

    lasting or laughing
    fatigue is tiring

trying to remove

This mis –

Confusing, confessing to not
knowing the blind contours

of sound, the map

from the page

or the crown from

the order

(of circumstance and odd chance)

I

That it would begin like this

water calling from
under a bridge
                    Words

in an Italian notebook
from a century ago –

                    or several

She says thank you for

It is so late that we may be too early
for the next century

Which you say may never come
in our lifetime,

                    of loss

is found
in the water the reason of solstice
or solace

Next to a soulless iron gate
you beg
          to be

Let in

on the joke that is a life
without a line

          to hold

the lineage leading from heretic to heretic
to hypocrisy

          This

trying too hard
to say, in simple words

That there are none, but left
                    in traces

The impressions of too heavy hand
on the next page

              Blank   Why

it could have been the water, or
a glass smile

forming a mirror in which
you see you and not the flesh

of kin less kind nor king
this search

              While searching straight past

The obvious intrudes
in rude awakenings of not
so simple sleep

              This peace less push

Beyond water, is a memory
or dream

              lapsed held in motion's place
              of being

You will not say
that you do not know
What

              is knowledge

Ripped on the edge

          as footsteps

annoyingly close yet too fast

          This current trying

to catch the tide
between each

       wave, is

another without a time
to call as its own

         This legacy

limping from
story to story is the villa

       or villain
       you run past

without seeing what arose
is a garden near a river

       from which
       you could not drink

in the landscape
so perfect in the sound

       of trees

or there, leaves
holding the secret of what falls

caught

Just beyond vision

        your seeing
        the meaning

of this conversation in tongues

The sages spoke of fountains
more dangerous than men

whose war
is behind us

        Yet peace
        is

Passable the routes of ancient caravans
take us by the knees needing a thrashing

To cut through mistaken divinity leaving
clearing is a chore

        left to do

In between the times

        of war
        is war, again

It is the sight of blood which becomes before

The smell opens out
into an empty expanse of remembrance

        for those who have fallen

Rising in the flowering wing

etched, as an artificial limb

left holding
flight as flight

itself is the sound of reason

For the crown, it became common
to assume the general good

of the people

is served this banquet to which
none are invited

But called nonetheless
is treason, the

Treasury of ship is a sunken hold

held

in the belonging wreckage
in the very act of voyage
is the imposter imposing

flag Sure

of what

it was wrote to reassure
reassess

A very certain frailness

This fable of forgotten chateau

Hollow in the halls are none

but mirrors

Reflecting back the primordial palace
Gilded in row after row of hammered

steal
if one must

These precious moments

prodigal for their
markings, a life

Lined with frayed circumscription

of the continual scroll
from which erasure

Is being led chapeau by chapeau to

the head of a pavilion in the park in the square

Rounded by
endless night

Forms
the shadow

of what was marked

As the final date, the year after
the hyphen on the stone heading

The grave is not

expansion, this separating
in early hour

    where the fog
    will not do

To mask the pains covered
in night's reunion

    Still, the rose

pushes the instance of history

        forward

Towards an open door, unhinging

        all of

would not be sufficient to make
a quietness last

     beyond its own insistence

of not being

held in the bosom of friendship
is the loss of lands

     unrecovered in battle

Shifts the focus from inner gardens

to outer courts of walled in cities

Where you could breathe became

        The light curious in reflected
        season's slant

of time the measure is taken
        And then quickly lost

This path of rose
        would just as simply
        smelled of sweet wax

a candle chandelier

        Near a coliseum in glass
Resistance of sentries

        at the arch
        of bowed circumstance

is found destiny
straightening vision through branches
of trees

        We fell out

of sight in perspective

        this certain
        trick

of holding distance

        even closer

than the canvas at hand

is surely an excuse

    for the falling of waters
    on a platform with trap doors

Opening onto the ledge
      where you step into frame

Sure of the space
      the codes
      and secret knowledges

of vows etched upon shields

       the light from eclipse
       or ellipse

upon the lips of kings

    Being called

into question the night

     Braces for the day
     And leaves stars for sailors

    to follow

   ₜyou choose not the route

which flowed from the bells

in the village church now turned
garden said the royal

    Blew in the face

A wind in rows
of chestnuts, lavenders and pearl

                         This precious
                         Recall
between each broken
memory seized in endless white

      when color fades in uniform

division of ruins

       the lasting out paces the beginning

in simple voyage toward
unknown water
               is a moment shared in
               unrecognized treaties

upon the same floor, a ground
of unspilled blood,   in unison

      sung just above

were the hills upon which

        peace was promised

not so much as reward
but as in   idea

      the matter was formed

to push surface

      Between each

Season was another time

A time which called place

      to be none other than the moment

That is was believed
was the curse cast

      among the poplars
      and the people

in plain suppliance leaping from

      prince to price

A pawn was bought

      for the sacrifice

of reason was waged in
unimaginable battles

      between each ledge
      was formed another

Legend rocking in the distance
as to trap a closeness in the regard back

through tiny openings
the water was let in

between each shimmering
a phantom more real

      stood the castle in stone

cold silence was the answer

from the court one could see
distances opening

    in to immense maps
    and perfect architectural plans

upon which the trees were planted
as reminders of the fruits
that for loss

    flowered as each human desire

left hungry in the eating

    was the principle for the banquet

around perfectly set tables
were infinities each with a back door

    closing in upon

the sight of all evil casting
eyes upon unvanquished lands or

    a mariner's quest

of open waters fleeing swords and taboos

    left unblemished in the breaking

of each wave was there found a pause

    for time

between time is nothing

but time

    for the taking

lands were surrendered
without armistice or

        Justice which was called
        farce, this fact

of being too close

        to one or another
        is definition for the seizure

of the riches found in the unburying

        of the dead or in the shadows

where more shadows opening upon

        engraved ornaments and gallows

such little disasters marked a life

        in simplicity's refusal

of the obvious complexities

        in the design

distance was reached

        branch by branch

the rivers met fountains, trees

        and the chase was readied

as men shook hands in preparation for the fight

a woman bared her breast

        while running

waters mounted just ahead

        in the distance was found
        new distances and deserts

where once stood mountains, monuments, and

        and sudden lights

filled newly vacant rooms

        where silence was the chalice
        from which one could drink

in all the beauties uncovered

        in the loss

of foreign territories less
their continual support

        of the apparent need

for silence words were created
as a man walks in the fog

        Around the bend
        is found another turn

at trying to rescue

        peace from the question posed

in still light or plain day

A plan was forged

    through the original play

of circumstance and odd chance

    was left in boundless steps
    across an otherwise empty

promises to fulfill uncertain

    roots of the trees they would become

without questioning the field
of certain logics locked

    in open site

the trigger was pulled
between each storm

    a glimpse of light was cut
    near a kiosk or cyclopes
    or newer versions of older tales

From which one could not escape
the insistent pounding or claps

of thunder announcing a different age
as appealing as bells masked

    the stems from the sound

of reason which rose

    to a deity deafening in reply

as tribes took to fire

　　　　Flowing in between ritual
　　　　and rite staircases crossed

rivers torturing quest

　　　　for the sea locked

in an embrace of dissipating steam

　　　　was found the power

Strengthening a bond
or breaking a note from a bank

　　　　　　of sound for a King
　　　　　　A ransom of random

thought around the ending
of eye wide wonder

　　　　Why you'll never be

other than this land or layers of water
A float upon a division of

　　　　　　sky and sea

upon which broader reaches were grasped
into empty caverns carried

　　　　as commerce of contrivance

you traversed such dark space

　　　　of non existent notice

as one given the time

      to leave or stay

put pressures upon fragile soils

      unturned in planting's loss

of fertile vision
in the haze of happenstance

on the closure of once open bounds

in the fury of thought's remembrance
      of thought

      was a way

Thinking through

      in place
      of place, put place

as time noted
each passing

      Away of being
      still

enough to give room

      To the rumors
      we would become

None other than this

      blind speculation

of what the hour meant

        A certain
        pressing down

against surer currents
        of time

        We trapped being
        just

for an instant, an insistence

of defying the natural order

        of numbers
        where none

Make sense of a logic that could not speak

           This music

a choir of choral cords
discorded in the tuning

        of each season's

Light was found
another's darkness

        or somber tones

in the music
of a language

        None could speak

for
or against

was art made

to seem impenetrable
in the very light

of too heavy words

Left hanging

in

intersections of prosaic
Response

of what this time
means given the

space between repetition
and pause

A world breaks
free of conflict in

to little pieces

Were left to place
hope upon the shoulders
borne in wildest tempest

of self forsaken lore
to behold
open expanses upon duckfilled ponds

Surviving certain

drought

This drink of longing

Filled in uncompromised
              space

Where the planets were
left spinning upon such fine

              threads

lightly falling each foot fall

follows another

to another

           Way of life let in

            between the imagined and the

unimaginable loss

           of never having

the means

to change this sentence

           in mid-sentence

Was hope made

           hopelessly caught in the

shortened space of time's

           look back into inverted

mirrors the image

That we see

        one another as the same

shift's back perspective

        from perspective's opening

into a field of

        light bounced darkness

from which we could not see

        land from sea

It was there
that islands became the strait

        You could not cross
        into open waters

to quench a thirst
for freedom's vanquished longing

        to be held

in the very bosom of reason

        is the illogical at home

    found in the unity
    of separation

You quest the contest

        but not the sight

of unwitnessed wholeness

        in momentary half tones

Your music
to another's song

        A perfect resonance
        in imperfect time

Marking a life in the permanence

        of the impermanence
        that is

This sentence.

(beckoning the waters)

II

Why in the looming

        half distance
        of the nearer

lost in the sound
this trying to hear

        a closer tone

        to be

The reasoning look into

        Looking back

is not moving forward

        this thrust into certain

        Stillness

outside of calm
Recalled sure

        or safe less

lost in the witnessing

        Why

        in the space of space
        you can see

        Straight through

to another space

Where

A little boy learns to jump

                    or new muscle
                    in the arms
at the outside
of war
                    And conquest
one might find

a hedge in fog near a man
with a pitch fork and reason

                    to be still
                    turning the Earth
It is as clear
as a question

impossible to answer

                    Why the old woman
                    pushes the baby

                    back into being

Such roundness
this existence

a simple smell
                    of onions
                    on a bus

And the wait near the fountain

Where you fall in

          love with aesthetics

And what was

Least wanted

        is wanted most

tightly held
in the escaping

        of breath
        are words

Made in too young
shaking hands

        Nonetheless

Open this closing in
vast scapes of
        Sky eyed
        wonder

wandering back and forth
in the narrow

        passage of time

times time
is less than a moment

        Missed in pure sun
        lit shadows

Through a tree

Where the tree is

        missing

The stillness of absence
is all

        That is left in the leaving

Leaning into a certain wind
blown wish winding up

        breathless

by the sea or grounded
in shells of sand

        melted into a mirror
        of reflection in

        still water

        deeply

held in open
hands

upon hands held
still

This always moving

Vision of what vision means

        without light
        is the darkest

Clearest

or closest

this thought of towers
of stone

        Thrown into pond
        Ripples by

And rips us
from the fabric
        of dream

This life
Why could be

        any other
        dream

if you must

Wonder why

life is

        No longer a wonder

just walking by
brushes seclusion

in the chill of morning

        A body lies
        Vacant

of thought
is thought

        held

Turning into distance

A mountain of rock

In a little girl's arms

       Climbs

into sound
of delirious water

       falling

inceaseably upon
too clean pavement

       to catch

this vision
of just glanced

       witnessing
can't help
but to miss

       fact

from friction
in rounder outer

       orbits

of non recall
Stretched beyond

       All limit

lies waiting

Hurried thoughts

        of war

invades a simple peace

        That is simply not

there a man
and woman carry a chair

           to a place of sun
And set
cloudlike

        This age
        that we have
despite protest
is destined

           not to last
The night
but to collide

          in open daylight

Revealing
  tulips at the outset and
  daisies in the end

          Could not defend

 the hip from spine
Nor belly from breast

        This simple test
        of birth

or death

can't help
but to define us

        a solemn twist
        undoing the door

from hinge to hinge
to hedge

        This ledge
        over looking

Heather and cliff
and brambles and bails

        us out

of bounds
        of production
        this headless, this heartless
being being
neither solitude
        nor solid
        yet awake

Near an open
give or takes
        us there

Where sky meets water
in an emptied hill

        emphatic in it loss

of voice
is voicing struck

        deaf by the release

of air and where

we are left tasting
rain or rose

          from the moments
          quiet inside
in between
At the very end of separation

          where vision fuses
          us from looking beyond
What mind
is mind made
          of flower
          or water or craft
One knows
No one
          all the better this bitter
          truth plus truthlessness

past all tests assembled
in this place or palace

          places pressures
          at the root

of injustices sprung
in the act of redress

          This night
          lost in love

in amplified sun
through tiny drops

          of water

Sprouting not
from without

These shared instances
of absolute reflection
                    Are shown again
                    and again

                    To be just
                    the image

of the image sought
is caught in the fleeting

                    concrete realizations that
                    you are

This flowing connection
lucid and solid
                    as water
                    mixed with air

gives rise to the fire
of unimaginable dust

                    falling without fail
                    upon the innocent and frail

Memories unearthed
in the turning of earth
                    to dust or rust
                    are we

          only the moment
          from moment

Profound and simple
and simply lost

                    in the hurry of
                    grand embarkments

Sliding into night sand
without stumble

      this close
      this far regard

Driving all sense
into the backward glance

        opening out
        from memories   attachment

into which we fall
head first into events

        or places held
        so tight
they vanish
or relinquish
        the anguish
        disguised as life

long past the time
where time cedes its hold

        beckoning the waters

to rise or fall again
begs the question of being
        Ready to pose

as a silhouette of
a statue in the distance

        Receding

after the fact
into the shadow of shock

or is it silence
which calls or calms

        As clearly as it began

it stalls then stops
the motion from the frame

        falls before the drop
off into sleep
is shattered

        by the sudden
Call
it if you wish
        a wish
or desire
to decide

        in open
        sunlight

blinding or blending
the image and the shadow

        with the fact
        and the remembrance

fused falsely
in the focus

        yet tightly held
        as a hope

to opt out
of space

        into even wider spaces

As if a tree
a rose   on the narrow
              banks

of a river
flows a thought

              Thoughtlessly cast

this shadow
of a man

              in the insistence of light

drowns the breath
in gulps of hallowed grasp

                        at the moment
                        pushed

into isolation
lashes and latches
                        on and on
                        we go

Stumbling forward into
history's end

              or do we

begin?

(pushing what flowers)

III

To see, is the ending lost
as ice flows
                    so us

into another time

                    where declarations
or declamations
erupt in erudite

                    emptiness
                    of hollowed out

warnings that there is

                    no time

to lose in the waiting
for dream simple

                    engagements

click, then lock
as if were
                    a question

to each statement's
purpose or suppose

                    it is position

Then what is the turning
into unanswerable question

                    is it
                    to be

held

In each moment's passing
Is what
                    found
fulfilled
in an instant

                    an instance
                    undivided

canceling time
for all time
                    bears no
                    witness

to this as what
is there
                    without doubt
                    it is

Nothing but
the certainty

                    that you are
                    not asking

This question falls between
the passing understanding

                    and the passive
                    resistance

Which begs form
to follow what

                    Will you be

is clear
the clarity of becoming

lost in the last
moment of grasping

                for air

is nothing
but you

        will not do
        what will

be done
in the last hour

        of searching
        for breath

Is rest
less peace

        Full of pause

in mid stride
between one

        And another
        wave

Is a goodbye heard
to be beckoning hello

        or just simply
        stopping

is a toll
pealing

        or appealing

to our basest
beliefs which

                    are best
                    laid bare

by very certain
uncertainties

                given
                what exactitudes

cover at best
partially

                  or is it
                partially best

in the cleaving
to remain divided

                for that is sure

as a nest around
is found a neck

                heading towards
                destruction as empty as

a sack full of wind
drives the break forward

                or forewarned
                is it forsaken

to long without breath
to fully breathe in

                The risk of living
                is found what

tempest in the calm
of recall

        in distance
        is it a test

teasing surety from stone
or blood from letting

        the air falls through
        What tiny openings

close in too tightly
to be rightly left
        Where
        you might have been

looking this way

        You asked

of the ripple
floating above the leaves

        yet grounded
        as upward rain

drops on rails

        against what

direction
is lost
        found aloft
        groundless without thought
was it
or was it not

        Noticed

The time passing

        on what was offered

is taken back
just as quickly

        sounds erupt
        Rupturing seamingless

tranquility is found
where

        There is nothing
        but what about that
is
where you are

        Where you are
        from

Moment to moment
a hat tossed into the air

        Astride next to an ancient wall
you sit
is it
        inside out or
        outside in

Apparent panic
peace flees

        itself
        back first

Pushed into
resonance

turning to face
the shear enormity

        of nothing
        is death

This
sure of
      facing time
      that passes

Barely

      Noticeable
      you asked again

in shadows
Is power

      hiding, abiding or
      lost

In that last
fitful shouting

        into what
is useful
      as a means

to a certain
ending
      badly as was begun
      again

Pushing
what flowers

      into or out of
      snow

White is the color
of loss
        as pale as
        a bucket

kicked over
the moon

        Spills what

is contained
in that absence

        of a very certain sense

that you are
not here   Or are
        hearing this
        or that

forms the will
of nothing

        Certain
        you asked
again
        or did you
        say

that you knew
How to tell

        the question
        from the answer

You reject
emptiness

As the gift
you wished

      wondering is it awe
      full to be

or to be not
so lost

      in the clear
      of a clearing

you hesitated

      to walk
      for fear of falling

Straight through
time you rushed

        after what
        is moving

Still
is the vibration

      of being

you. . .

ACKNOWLEDGMENTS

The author wishes to thank Guy Bennett, Jennifer K. Dick, Douglas Messerli, Sarah Riggs, Cole Swensen, Jim Wine, and Andrew Zawacki, the first readers of this text, whose input made it a better work. And a very special thank you to its publisher, Charles Alexander, both for his careful reading, comments, and loving care in taking this project into book form, and too for his own poetry which served as an initial source of inspiration for this work.

About the Author

Joe Ross is the author of over twelve books of poetry, most recently, *1000 Folds,* Chax Press, *Wordlick,* Green Integer Press (2011) and *Strata,* Dusie Press *(2008).* He has also published *Fractured // Connections . . . ,* bilingual Italian/English, La Camera Verde Press and *EQUATIONS = equals,* Green Integer Press, 2004. Former Literary Editor of the arts bi-monthly *The Washington Review* from 1991-1997, and co-founder of both the *In Your Ear* reading series in Washington, D.C. and the *Beyond the Page* reading series in San Diego, California, he received a National Endowment for the Arts Fellowship Award for his poetry in 1997 and is the three time winner of the Gertrude Stein Poetry Award in 2003, 2005, and 2006. He presently resides in Paris.

Other Books by the Author:

Guards of the Heart: Four Plays (Sun & Moon Press, 1990)
How to Write; or, I used to be in love with my jailer (Texture Press, 1992)
An American Voyage (Sun & Moon Press, 1993)
Push (Leave Books, 1994)
De-flections (Potes & Poets Press, 1994)
Full Silence (Upper Limit Music Press, 1995)
The Fuzzy Logic Series (Texture Press, 1996)
The Wood Series (Seeing Eye Books, 1997)
EQUATIONS =equals (Green Integer Press, 2004)
Strati (Bi-lingual Italian/English, La Camera Verde, 2007)
FRACTURED // Connections ... (Bi-lingual Italian/English, La
        Camera Verde, 2008)
Strata, (Dusie Press, 2008)
Wordlick (Green Integer, 2011)

About Chax Press

Chax Press is a 501(c)(3) nonprofit organization, founded in
1984, and has published more than 140 books, including fine art
and trade editions of literature and book arts works.

For more information, please see our web site at http://chax.org

Chax Press is supported by individual contributions, and by
the Tucson Pima Art Council and the Arizona Commision on
the Arts, with funds from the State of Arizona and the National
Endowment for the Arts.

 TUCSON PIMA
ARTS
COUNCIL

Arizona
Commission
on the Arts

NATIONAL
ENDOWMENT
FOR THE ARTS